GOSPEL 101 FOR TEENS:

Learning, Living, and Sharing the Gospel

Jeff Dodge

New
Growth
Press

newgrowthpress.com

New Growth Press, Greensboro, NC 27401
newgrowthpress.com
Copyright © 2024 by Jeff Dodge

Cover Design: Faceout Studio, adapted by Dan Stelzer
Interior Typesetting and eBook: Lisa Parnell, lparnellbookservices.com

ISBN: 978-1-64507-446-5 (Print)
ISBN: 978-1-64507-447-2 (eBook)

Library of Congress Cataloging-in-Publication Data on file

Printed in the United States of America

31 30 29 28 27 26 25 24   1 2 3 4 5

CONTENTS

INTRODUCTION

Evangelism is a scary word with a bad reputation. It might make some people think of a preacher yelling. Others might imagine someone handing out pamphlets on the street corner. Still others might think of a friend nervously fumbling over words like "sin" and "repent" while secretly looking around to make sure not too many people are listening in.

But what if *evangelism* just meant having a conversation in which we share the beautiful story of God's love in the gospel in a humble and simple way?

In this book, we're going to look at the gospel mainly as a story—a story that begins with God's perfect creation and ends with God's perfect new creation.

The hope is that what you learn will help you talk more comfortably and naturally about the good news of the Bible. My desire is for you to learn to communicate the gospel in a way that reflects how deep and meaningful it is, while at the same time making the message clear, understandable, and appealing.

To help you get there, I have three goals for this book:

1) *Gospel Familiarity.* You will get to know the language of the gospel. We will all spend a lifetime exploring the many dimensions of the gospel, but this book's focus will be on the "big picture" of the gospel—the heart of the message.

2. *Gospel Community.* Working through this book with others will enrich your study. It is amazing what your fellow students will teach you!

3. *Gospel Action.* The gospel message is not just to be studied; it is to be shared. This book will help you learn to have good gospel conversations with your unbelieving friends and family.

So grab your Bible (it's going to be your main textbook!), join your small group of friends and fellow students, and use this study as a guide to understanding the gospel better. This book won't give you and the others in your small group a magic formula for sharing with your friends, but it will give you new language and new angles you can use to talk naturally about the gospel in everyday conversations.

My hope is that your time with your group will help you want to share this good news with the waiting world!

HOW TO USE THESE SESSIONS

Studying the Bible in community with others is important. Why? One reason is that if you only study your Bible alone, it will be easy for you to go in the wrong direction. We often need others to help us stay on track. God has connected us to each other through the Spirit to bring balance and help to our understanding. Because of that, you'll be doing the readings and activities for each session as a group.

There are five parts to each session.

First, you will look at a short *introduction* to the topic of the week.

Second, you will do a *Bible reading* that will encourage you to interact with God's Word. This time of learning from the Bible is the most important part of your time together.

Third, you will read an *article* that will give you a broader understanding of the topic from the Bible reading. Here and there in the book, you will see a word in **bold**. You will find this word explained in a "Words to Know" section at the end of the article in the session where the word appears.

Fourth, you can process what you learned from the Bible passages and the article by answering the *discussion questions* together.

Finally, in most sessions you will be encouraged to *survey* two people during the week in order to connect what you are learning with what real people out in the world are thinking. The surveys are very short— no more than a few questions. The next time you meet with your small group, you will share what you learned from the survey and hear what others learned.

Then you'll begin the next session in the book.

This goal of this book is to present an overview of the gospel message, to invite you to begin to wrestle with some of the questions that arise as you think about and discuss the gospel, and to get you started on finding your own ways to share your faith with others.

Diving into a study of the gospel helps make us humble. That humility helps put us in the right frame of mind for worshipping God. And humility is just what we need when we share our faith with others. As you work through this book, let the gospel truths go deep into your soul. Stop often to praise God in gratitude, and let your joy overflow to others. Studying the gospel leads to worship. We see this in Paul's letter to the Romans. In the first eleven chapters, Paul gets into some deep theology as he explains various aspects of the gospel. Then, after all that heavy lifting, it's as though he pushes the chair back from his desk, throws his hands in the air, and with tearful joy exclaims, "Oh, the depth of the riches both of the wisdom and knowledge of God!" (Romans 11:33 NKJV).

TIPS FOR CONDUCTING YOUR SURVEYS

Purpose

- The purpose of these surveys is to *listen* to people and *learn from* them.
- You might hear some things that bother you or that contradict what you've been learning. However, the purpose of these surveys is *not* to debate. If someone's perspective differs from yours, it's even more important to listen well to understand what they're saying. Hear them out. When they are done, you should be able to explain back to them what you have heard them say—without adding in changes of your own.
- If the person is open to having a longer conversation, then of course you may kindly and gently share what you've been learning. But if they'd rather not get into a longer conversation, humbly respect their wishes. Again, your goal is to *listen* and to *learn*.
- If they ask you a question and you're not sure of the answer, it's okay to say, "I don't know!" Maybe you can find someone later who can help you with an answer.

People

- You're looking for two people to survey each week.
- When you ask someone if they'd be willing to do answer a few questions for a survey you're conducting, explain that it's for a course that you're doing about the story of the Bible.
- Don't assume that people will be up for doing the surveys—even if they're your friends. Ask them if they're willing, and if they say no, move on to someone else.
- Ideally, you'd talk to the same people each week, but if the same people aren't available each week, look for someone who is available and willing.

- It would be great if you're able to talk to people who come from outside your church because their perspectives might be different, giving you an opportunity to learn.
- It's probably better to take these surveys to people you already know so that conversations can develop over the entire time you're in this course.

Practical Matters

- You might want to ask your survey question(s), sit back and listen carefully, and then write down what you remember from your conversation when you're done.
- Or you might want to take some notes while the other person is speaking so that you don't forget what they said.
- Or maybe you'll find it easiest to record the person's answers on your phone. Before doing this, though, you should make sure the person is comfortable being recorded. And you still might want to make a few notes later to have with you when it's time to share your survey results with your group.

Prayer

- You can never go wrong praying before you enter into a conversation! Pray for humility. Pray that you would listen carefully and patiently. Pray for the ability to keep from interrupting. And pray that God would bless the people you're hearing from and the time you're spending together.

SEEING THE STORY OF THE GOSPEL

INTRODUCTION

Read this introduction aloud as a group (2–3 minutes).

Why the Gospel Matters

Christians talk a lot about the "gospel."

What does that mean? The word *gospel* means "good news." But knowing that is just the beginning.

In its fullest, richest form, the gospel is a story. In fact, it's *the* Story—the true story the Bible tells that makes sense of all the other stories we've heard. It's the story that makes sense of life itself.

In some ways, of course, the Bible contains many stories. After all, it's made up of sixty-six books written across many centuries by many different authors.

But as you get to know it better, you'll see how the thread of the gospel is woven through all of those books so that together they tell one Big Story.

We find the first whispers of the gospel in the opening pages of the first book of the Bible, Genesis, and then we see it unfold until we get to the last words of the last book, Revelation.

One reason we can talk freely to people about the gospel is that something about it resonates with us as humans. Most people have a nagging feeling that there is something beyond this world. Why? Because deep down, we crave unending, unconditional love and the sure promise of a better tomorrow. These longings show that people are hardwired to seek answers only the gospel provides.

We find traces of these longings and hints of the hope of the gospel in many of the fictional stories we've heard over the course of our lives, whether in books or TV shows or movies or songs. Think about how much people love figures like Gandalf and Dumbledore, who are wise and caring, yet also powerful—or heroes like Aragorn and Katniss Everdeen, who stand for what's right against the forces of evil. Think about how satisfying it is to see bad guys overthrown, whether it's Sauron or Voldemort or Thanos. Think about the hurt and bitterness we hear in songs about love gone wrong. And then think about all the happy endings in all the rom-coms out there. Even the popularity of dystopian fiction reflects our desire for things that are wrong to be made right. We can't escape our longings for peace and safety and justice and love. Is it possible that we fill our screens and earbuds with stories that point us to the Big Story—the gospel? And so maybe when we hear the gospel, something about it sounds familiar to us. We recognize it and embrace it.

That's the hope behind *Gospel 101 for Teens*. It's intended to help you and others see the Story that is central to the Bible and that makes sense of the world the way no other story can. And one more thing (spoiler alert): the hero-king at the center of it is Jesus.

Reading

Read the Bible passages together (4–6 minutes).

As you read, think about this question: What do these verses tell us about the gospel or *good news*? You may wish to jot down some notes below.

- **Romans 1:1–5, 15–17**

  Our basic calling "grace & apostleship"
  [sin = death
  gift of God = eternal life

- **Romans 6:23**

- **1 Corinthians 15:1–5**

  · By the gospel you are saved if you hold firmly to the word
  He died for our sins, was buried, raised on the 3rd day, appeared to Peter & the Twelve

- **Revelation 14:6–7**

  ... eternal gospel to proclaim on earth – to every nation, tribe, language and people.
  "Fear God and give him glory, because the hour of his judgment has come. Worship him who made the heavens, the earth, the sea & springs of water."

What do these verses tell us about the gospel or good news?

Notes:

ARTICLE

Read this article aloud as a group (9–12 minutes).

For some of you, a few of the Bible passages you just read contained words you expected to hear in a discussion of the gospel: *sin, salvation, faith, eternal life,* and of course *Jesus.*

But did one of those passages seem a little different from the others?

For me, it was the last one, the one from Revelation.

Let's look at it again: "Then I saw another angel flying in midair, and he had the eternal gospel to proclaim to those who live on the earth—to every nation, tribe, language and people. He said in a loud voice, 'Fear God and give him glory, because the hour of his judgment has come. Worship him who made the heavens, the earth, the sea and the springs of water'" (Revelation 14:6–7 NIV).

The flying angel who's proclaiming "the eternal gospel" certainly grabbed my attention. But it was something else that really got me thinking: Where's Jesus? If someone is proclaiming the gospel, shouldn't Jesus be in there?

From these two verses, I zoomed out to take a look at the whole book of Revelation. The entire book is "the revelation of Jesus Christ" (Revelation 1:1). The angel didn't forget that Jesus is at the center of the gospel message. But in chapter 14, the angel proclaims parts of the gospel that often get left out.

It dawned on me that what was being proclaimed was a gospel that spans from the *beginning* of the world—the creation—to the judgment at the *end* of the world. The gospel is the storyline that ties the whole Bible together!

This *aha* moment sent me on a journey through the Bible. As I explored, a few cover-to-cover aspects of the gospel story became clearer to me and made Jesus's role in it even more wonderful. Here are three themes that stood out:

1. THE GOSPEL IS THE TRUE STORY OF GOD'S KINGDOM

The angel's gospel focuses our eyes on the God who is the Creator of the universe. When the angel refers to "the one who made heaven and earth," that takes us from the last book of the Bible back to the account of creation at the beginning of the Bible in Genesis.

Consider everything God created as his kingdom. The idea of God's kingdom appears on page after page of the Bible, and the grand finale is the crowning of Jesus as the supreme King of all at the end of Revelation.

When an idea starts at the very beginning of a book and keeps appearing all the way up to the very end, it means we should pay attention to it. Although God used many human writers to write the many books of the Bible, he is the true Author who planned out the whole storyline to give us the complete good news of the gospel.

We've seen some of the ways that books and movies and songs echo parts of the gospel. Think about it: if you take a sweeping, birds-eye view of the best storylines and look for a pattern, I think you'll find an uncanny similarity to the storyline of the Bible:

- First, there's a kingdom whose peace and harmony are suddenly shattered. The kingdom falls into enemy hands. This is like the perfect creation and the **fall** into sin in Genesis 1–3.
- The plot thickens. Things go from bad to worse. Then a hero-king appears on the scene. At the high point of the story, the hero-king

takes on the bad guy and wins the victory. This part of the story is like Genesis 4 through Revelation 20, in which God works out his plan of salvation. The high point is Jesus's death, resurrection, and ascension.

- Finally, the heroism of the hero-king brings peace and harmony back to the kingdom. We see this beautifully restored kingdom in Revelation 21–22.

It's as if God has put an antenna in us to pick up the signals pointing us to this epic storyline. As we go about our lives, we sense that something is wrong. We long for the peace of a restored kingdom. God has written—and starred in—this epic narrative, and traces of it are all around us.

2. THE GOSPEL CENTERS ON THE TRUE HERO-KING, JESUS

The coming of a hero-king was the long-awaited hope of God's kingdom. Listen to Jesus's grand announcement when he finally steps onto the scene: "The time is fulfilled, and the kingdom of God has come near. **Repent** and believe the good news!" (Mark 1:15).

Later, Paul picks up on this theme in his letter to the Romans. He gives us a glimpse of the overarching storyline of the Bible and highlights Jesus's role as hero. Take a look at how he starts and finishes his letter:

> Paul, a servant of Christ Jesus, called to be an apostle and set apart for the gospel of God—*the gospel he promised before-hand through his prophets in the Holy Scriptures* regarding his Son, who as to his earthly life was a descendant of David, and who through the Spirit of holiness was appointed the Son of God in power by his resurrection from the dead: *Jesus Christ our Lord.* (Romans 1:1–4 NIV, emphasis added)

Now to him who is able to strengthen you according to my gospel and the proclamation about Jesus Christ, *according to the revelation of the mystery kept silent for long ages but now revealed and made known through the prophetic Scriptures,* according to the command of the eternal God to advance the obedience of faith among all the Gentiles—to the only wise God, through Jesus Christ—to him be the glory forever! Amen. (Romans 16:25–27, emphasis added)

Humanity has fallen, and the earth is not as it should be. But wait—that's not the end of the story! The gospel proclaims that the Hero-King Jesus has returned to his kingdom!

3. THE GOSPEL CALLS FOR US TO RESPOND

Remember that *gospel* means "good news." As news, it's a message we are to tell other people. And the news is good because the King whose realm we live in is coming and wants us to know him and enjoy his presence.

Such big news demands a response. Not just a thumbs-up. We need to *do* something! What do we need to do? Jesus tells us in Mark 1:15: "Repent and believe the good news!"

The world is a mess. And we are part of the problem. Sometimes we hurt others. Sometimes we're careless with the beautiful creation God has given us. Sometimes we ignore the true King and carry on with our lives as if he had never come.

So we need to hear this good news! When we do, we have a choice. We can ignore the King and suffer the consequences of sticking with the mess of the fallen world. Or we can repent and join the One who has come to restore the kingdom. When we accept that he's the King, we find new life as citizens in the harmonious realm he's establishing.

The world is messed up. It's very good news that it won't always be that way, and that we can join the new kingdom and be part of helping it grow.

THE TAKEAWAY

This has been just a short introduction to the gospel, but I hope it has helped you see the beauty of its message and its Hero, Jesus.

If you have already believed this gospel, you can begin to proclaim the good news of the King and his kingdom. What might that look like? At home, you can remind your family how the struggles we experience are very real—but are ultimately resolved by our true King. When you're together with other Christians, you can remind one another that following Jesus means acknowledging that he is the King, and you can ask whether there are any areas of your life where the King doesn't seem to have the influence he should have. In your classroom or at your job, you can agree with those around you that the world really is broken, but you can also let them see that you have hope that "the kingdom of God is near"—and you can invite them to join you in that hope by repenting and believing.

WORDS TO KNOW

The fall: Adam and Eve's disobedience in the garden of Eden. God had forbidden Adam and Eve to eat the fruit from one tree (out of many). After the serpent—Satan—tempted Eve, she and Adam both ate. As a result, sin, death, and suffering entered the world, and Adam and Eve were forced to leave the garden.

Repent: When we repent, we turn around. We turn *away from wrong things* that we've done or said or thought, and *away from our failure* to do or say or think good things. We turn *toward God* in faith, asking his forgiveness and his help as we seek change in our lives.

DISCUSSION

Group members should take 5–6 minutes to look over the questions individually. Then the group should discuss the questions together (10 minutes).

1. What did you learn about the gospel from the readings in this lesson?

2. If someone asked you the question "What is the gospel?" how would you answer?

3. The article highlighted three points about the gospel. How many can you remember? Fill in the blanks below. (It's okay to go back and check!)

The gospel _is the true story of Gods Kingdom_

_____

The gospel _centers on the true Hero-king of_

Jesus

The gospel _calls us to respond_

_____

4. Which of these three points resonates with you the most? Why?

5. Why do you think it's often hard for Christians to talk about Jesus with the same eagerness they might have when they share other good news?

6. What might help you with your fears and insecurities in talking about Jesus? Consider Bible verses you know, or think about how what you have read today might help.

SURVEY

Survey two or three people by asking them the two questions below. Before beginning your conversations, review "Tips for Conducting Your Surveys" (p. 4). You will share what you found out the next time your group meets.

Write the answers people give you in the spaces below.

Person #1

Have you ever read the Bible?

What would you say the main message of the Bible is?

Person #2

Have you ever read the Bible?

What would you say the main message of the Bible is?

Person #3

Have you ever read the Bible?

What would you say the main message of the Bible is?

Notes for Yourself:

What did you learn from your survey?

What connections do you see between the survey responses and the article or Scriptures you've been studying?

LETTING GOD INTRODUCE HIMSELF: PART ONE

SHARING TIME (*10 minutes*)

Have group members share what they learned from the surveys they conducted over the past week.

- Do you notice any common themes in what group members heard?
- What connections do you see between survey answers and what you are learning in this study?

INTRODUCTION

Read this introduction aloud as a group (2–3 minutes).

Why Starting with God Matters

Sometimes our impressions of people are way off. Has this ever happened to you? A friend tells you all about a person they know. Then you meet the person and discover they're not like your friend described them at all! There's nothing like actually getting to know someone for yourself. Giving people the opportunity to introduce themselves is much better than taking someone else's word for it.

When it comes to God, we have heard a lot about him. People have all sorts of ideas and opinions about God. How can we know what's true?

We should let God introduce himself to us.

And God does a pretty good job of telling us about himself in the opening chapters of Genesis, which we'll look at in this session and the next. Plus, in Scripture's first few chapters, God sets the stage for the whole rest of the Bible—that grand Big Story we talked about in the last lesson. We can't skip too quickly past these all-important pages.

In doing these readings, you might find out that God isn't exactly like what you thought. So take your time now, and let God introduce himself to you.

You can even ask him, *God, is there anything you'd like us to know about you?*

Reading

Read the Bible passages together (4–6 minutes).

Tip: If these passages are already familiar to you, try to read them as if this is your first time ever seeing them.

As you read, think about these questions: What do these passages tell me about God? What do these passages tell me about humanity? You may wish to jot down some notes below.

- **Genesis 1:1–10**

  It's the grand Creator of all good things.

- **Genesis 1:11–28**

  He didn't just create the bare bones – He spoke into creation growing things, life, vegetation; the seasons; creatures – wild animals and livestock (v. 24–25)

- **Genesis 2:4–25**

  He gave 2 responsibilities to man – to work the garden + to name the animals

What do these passages tell me about God?

Notes:

He is the Creator of all Good Things; He Created us and the living world around us.

What do these passages tell me about humanity?

Notes:

We were given jobs intially - to work the garden and name the animals

Given "green plants" for food.

Just one "rule" - not to eat from the tree of ^the knowledge of good and evil.

ARTICLE

Read this article aloud as a group (9–12 minutes).

If you are reading a story, it's hard to make sense of it unless you understand the plot. You need to understand who the main characters are and where the whole story is going. That is also true of the story of our lives! If we don't understand the main characters in our own story—if we don't understand where we came from and where we're going—we have no hope of understanding ourselves or our world.

The gospel starts at the beginning of the Bible and gives us what we need to know to understand the story of our lives. Surprise! It turns out that the main character in our story is not us—it's God.

In the opening pages of Genesis, we find an attention-grabbing account of God calling his world into existence and making his most precious creation, human beings. As God brings the whole world into being, we see his great power; and as he cares for the humans he makes, we see his great love. All this sets the stage for the rest of the story of the gospel to unfold.

GOD: LOVING CREATOR

It is easy to read quickly through the opening of Genesis and miss something significant. God had a totally blank canvas to work with and no one telling him what he could and could not do. He could have done anything! This means that what he did was exactly what he wanted to do. It was 100 percent intentional!

God created everything out of nothing. All he had to do was speak, and creation snapped into existence. Sun! Moon! Water!

But when we get to God's crowning achievement—human beings—we see something different. And that difference is important. God didn't just speak from a distance; he "formed" Adam with his own hands and "breathed the breath of life into his nostrils" (Genesis 2:7). Likewise, he personally crafted Eve. By giving us such details, Genesis highlights God's tender love for humans.

We see this love again in the incredible home God set up for Adam and Eve. God went far beyond giving them what they needed to survive. The garden of Eden was a place of beauty and abundance, with flowering trees, many resources, biological diversity—so much to see and smell and touch and taste. In these verses, you can see God's love and joy as he gives humanity these plentiful gifts.

And because of this great love, God had a wonderful plan for what humans would do in his newly created world. Look at Genesis 1:26–28:

> Then God said, "Let us make man in our image, according to our likeness. They will rule the fish of the sea, the birds of the sky, the livestock, the whole earth, and the creatures that crawl on the earth."
>
> So God created man
> in his own image;
> he created him in the image of God;
> he created them male and female.
>
> God blessed them, and God said to them, "Be fruitful, multiply, fill the earth, and subdue it. Rule the fish of the sea, the birds of the sky, and every creature that crawls on the earth."

God is the all-powerful Creator, but he gave humans tremendous authority. They have the task of ruling creation wisely—"to work it and watch over it"—caring for what God made (Genesis 2:15). We see

Relationships of humans and animals

this authority again when God gives Adam the honor of naming every living creature (see Genesis 2:19).

God demonstrated his role as loving Creator by giving people incredible authority and everything they needed to flourish. What potential there was for humanity!

GOD: SUPREME AUTHORITY

It makes sense to us that if you create something, you're in charge of it. And in Genesis 1–2 we see God demonstrate his supreme authority by putting everything in order just the way he wanted it.

In creating the world, God started with nothing. Before he got to work, the earth had no shape or form; it was empty and dark (Genesis 1:2). Then, like a master architect, God began to put things in order. He separated the light from the darkness and the water from the land.

Then God made humans as the high point of creation. But even if they are the high point, they are still under his supreme authority. We see God's authority over the humans when he puts boundaries on what they can and can't do: "And the LORD God commanded the man, 'You are free to eat from any tree of the garden, but you must not eat from the tree of the knowledge of good and evil, for on the day you eat from it, you will certainly die'" (Genesis 2:16–17).

God lovingly gave humanity amazing freedom and a special place of honor, but there were limits. God had ordered creation perfectly. He was in charge, and humans would flourish only under his supreme authority. Going against his will would mean choosing death.

Under God's authority, Adam and Eve enjoyed a perfect relationship with God and each other. They knew who they were and experienced dignity and joy in ruling God's creation. Everything was set up for humans to do much more than just survive—they would thrive under

God's loving rule. God's kingdom was in a state of *shalom*, the perfect peace of life as it should be.

THE TAKEAWAY

By looking at the creation of humankind, we begin to get a picture of God's character, and we see the starting point of the plotline of the whole Bible—the gospel. God is our loving Creator who holds authority over our lives and over everything else he has made. God meant for human beings to thrive and experience relationship with him and joy in the world.

Now, we know that the world we live in is not like that—it is very much *not* as it should be. How did we get from Eden, that place of beauty and harmony, to where we are now? This is what we will explore in our next session as we turn the corner from Genesis 1 and 2 to Genesis 3.

But God's character has not changed. He is still loving. And his desire for people has not changed. He still seeks to bless them and bring them into relationship with him.

As you interact with your family and friends this week, look for ways you can begin to introduce them to this loving, blessing God—or ways you can get to know him better together.

DISCUSSION

Group members should take 5–6 minutes to look over the questions individually. Then the group should discuss the questions together (10 minutes).

1. In Genesis 1–2, God sets the stage for how we understand him and ourselves. What elements do you see in these opening chapters that are important to understanding the gospel?

2. What two aspects of God does the article highlight based on Genesis 1–2?

God: _Loving Creator_

God: _Supreme Authority_

What other aspects of God did you notice as you read the Genesis passage?

The freedom he gave man

3. Is there one of these aspects of God that you don't think about much? If so, which one?

The job He gave us?

4. Why is it important for us to see both God's love and God's authority?

5. What special role did God give humans in the world he had just created?

work the garden and obey Him (his guidance)

6. How does God's authority over humans naturally flow from the fact that he is our loving Creator?

SURVEY

We will conduct a survey about God's character after we study Genesis 3 next time. File away what you've learned about God this week so that you have it in your mind later.

LETTING GOD INTRODUCE HIMSELF: PART TWO

INTRODUCTION

Read this introduction aloud as a group (2–3 minutes).

That Sinking Feeling

Have you ever been watching a movie or reading a book, and you start to get a sinking feeling that the main character is about to do something dumb? You just *know* what's going to happen before it even plays out. Whatever they're about to do will ruin a relationship. Or destroy the new car they just got. Or harm an innocent person. Or bring catastrophe down on their own head. And you want to yell at them, "Don't do it!"

Last session, we saw that God is our loving Creator and supreme authority. We saw the goodness of the world he made and the beauty of the home he gave Adam and Eve in the garden of Eden. Everything was perfect—literally. Adam and Eve were at peace with God and with each other. They were experiencing life—as it should be—in God's glorious kingdom.

Yet something was about to go terribly wrong. Humans had been given a special place within this kingdom, under the authority of the King, but soon their bad decisions would cause this perfect harmony to come crashing down.

Reading

Read the Bible passage together (4–6 minutes).

Review: As their loving Creator, God gave Adam and Eve more than they would ever need for a happy, fulfilling life. He gave them just one restriction: "You are free to eat from any tree of the garden, but you must not eat from the tree of the knowledge of good and evil, for on the day you eat from it, you will certainly die" (Genesis 2:16–17).

Two tips: First, in this reading the serpent is Satan, or the devil. Second, if this passage is already familiar to you, try to read it as if this is your first time ever seeing it.

As you read, think about these questions: How is the picture the serpent gives of God different from what we've seen of God's character in Genesis 1 and 2? What does this passage tell me about humanity? You may wish to jot down some notes below.

- **Genesis 3**

She says "you mustn't touch (or eat) it"

How is the picture the serpent gives of God different from what we've seen of God's character in Genesis 1 and 2?

Notes:

*Bending truth – speaking falsehood
against God's word
• For the 1st time found shame ...
• He also named
• Then Eve blames God!
Hyperbole → ... (v. 16, 2:24)*

*Even in their disobedience, God cares for them – "made clothes"
v. 22 – the whole world order has been overturned*

What does this passage tell me about humanity?

Notes:

That even when we have all that we need, we will push the boundaries of disobedience

ARTICLE

Read this article aloud as a group (9–12 minutes).

We've talked about how in order to understand the story of our lives, we need to see that the main character in our story is actually God. We also need to understand that we ourselves and our entire world are the products of God's loving creativity.

But as we look at the world we live in, we see that it is very different from the one described in Genesis 1 and 2. That difference raises questions in our minds. The world of Genesis 1 and 2 was perfect, and everyone was happy. Where did suffering come from? And death? And broken relationships? And things big and small that just go wrong for no apparent reason?

In Genesis 3 we find the answer. Humans were created to live under God's supreme authority, according to his loving wisdom, and under his careful protection. Living under God's rule, Adam and Eve had not only perfect joy but also meaningful work: to bless the rest of creation as God had blessed them. But then they turned against God's good authority and tried to make the world run in a way it was never meant to run—with themselves in charge instead of the God who created it all.

Why did Adam and Eve give in to the temptation to disobey God, their Creator and friend?

The tree of the knowledge of good and evil was certainly "good for food and delightful to look at" (Genesis 3:6), so that's part of why its fruit was so tempting. But there were so many wonderful trees in the garden, all bearing delicious fruit. There's something else going on here.

The serpent, Satan, is "cunning" (Genesis 3:1) and deceptive. First, he causes Eve to doubt God's word. He flat-out lies, saying that they will *not* die if they eat the fruit. Then he introduces a new idea: God isn't blessing them as much as they thought he was; he's actually holding out on them. If you eat the fruit, the serpent says, "your eyes will be opened and you will be like God, knowing good and evil" (Genesis 3:5). Wow! To be like God . . . this idea captivates Eve. She sees the fruit in a new way, as "desirable for obtaining wisdom" (Genesis 3:6).

Adam and Eve—though under God's kind authority—have been given rule over all the rest of creation. But they think it's not enough. They want to "be like God."

So they eat.

Once they reject God and his authority, the beauty and harmony of the world are corrupted, and the peace and safety of the kingdom shattered.

And then they must face God's just judgment.

GOD: FINAL JUDGE

Adam and Eve directly disobeyed God's one and only command. God had told them plainly, *Don't eat from the tree or you will die.* Sadly, they did it anyway.

Adam and Eve didn't trust that God wanted what was best for them. They thought they could get something better, and they turned their backs on God. And as with all choices, there were consequences. God made the world. It belongs to him. The only rule he made for Adam and Eve had been broken. Independence from God sounded good to Adam and Eve—but it led to sorrow, brokenness, and death.

The consequences were immediate. God had come to the garden as their friend, to walk "at the time of the evening breeze" (Genesis 3:8)— but now he became their judge. Any good judge must be just. And so it was good and necessary for God, our kind and loving Creator, to carry out perfect justice.

What were the consequences of disobedience? For the woman, the birth of a child, which is supposed to bring great joy, would cause great pain, reminding us that all is not as it should be. For the man, the once joyful work of caring for a lush garden would become painful labor. God would send them both into exile, away from Eden, where they had lived in God's presence. And instead of living forever, all humans would die and become dust.

But did you pick up on the glimmer of hope in this hard chapter?

Even as God hands out perfect justice, he offers hope. He tells the serpent, "I will put hostility between you and the woman, and between your offspring and her offspring. *He will strike your head*, and you will strike his heel" (Genesis 3:15, emphasis added).

The judgment on humanity for the first sin was heavy. But in Genesis 3:15, God gives us a hint of his plan to ultimately CRUSH the serpent. One day, a human—a descendant of Eve—will strike the head of the serpent, defeating evil forever. This is an early glimpse of how the story will end. God doesn't abandon his broken world. Evil and sadness don't win in the end. Instead, God in his lovingkindness sends a Savior— Jesus, the offspring of Adam and Eve—to destroy sin and death forever.

We still experience the pain and the death that followed Adam and Eve's decision to go their own way. Sometimes living in our broken world feels like living in exile far from Eden. But through Jesus, God has made a way to bring us back home.

THE TAKEAWAY

In discussing stories and books in school, you've probably talked about *conflict*. Genesis 3 shows us the most disastrous conflict the world has ever known. Like Adam and Eve, people today still try to live outside of God's love and authority. And the consequences of doing that are still awful.

But God could see the end of the Big Gospel Story from the beginning. That is why he was able to give a hint about the coming of Jesus all the way back in the third chapter of Genesis. He was already planning to provide lost humans a way back to him. And he already had in mind the glorious resolution and restoration he would bring out of this catastrophe.

This is the story God has invited us into. This is the message you can bring to others.

DISCUSSION

Group members should take 5–6 minutes to look over the questions individually. Then the group should discuss the questions together (10 minutes).

1. Why is Genesis 3 important for understanding the gospel?

2. Fill in the final blank to see all three aspects of God we have discussed based on Genesis 1–3.

God: Loving Creator
God: Supreme Authority
God: _Final Judge_____

3. In our look at Genesis 3, we have spotlighted God's role as Judge. But God is always still the loving Creator and the supreme authority. What does God say and do in Genesis 3 that shows he is still the loving Creator? What does God say and do in Genesis 3 that shows he is still the supreme authority?

There are repercussions of their actions (evictions from Eden)

4. Do you think much about God as Judge? Why do you think it is good for us to remember that God is our final, ultimate Judge?

5. How does the Genesis 3 part of the gospel story connect to your home, school, work, and neighborhood? How has it affected our whole world?

SURVEY

Survey two or three people by asking them the questions below. Before beginning your conversations, review "Tips for Conducting Your Surveys" (p. 4). You will share what you found out the next time your group meets.

Write the answers people give you in the spaces below.

Person #1

Do you believe in God?

If yes, describe God. If no, why not?

Person #2

Do you believe in God?

If yes, describe God. If no, why not?

Person #3

Do you believe in God?

If yes, describe God. If no, why not?

Notes for Yourself:

What did you learn from your survey?

What connections do you see between the survey responses and the article or Scriptures you've been studying?

Consider this:

- If any of the people you surveyed said, "Yes, I believe in God," review the way they described God. Does their description resemble the way God introduces himself in Genesis, or is it different?
- The majority of the time, when people say, "No, I don't believe in God," they have a reason. Review how they answered the question *Why not?* to see if anything they say reminds you of what you learned in Genesis 1–3.

SEEING PEOPLE AS THEY ARE

INTRODUCTION

Read this introduction aloud as a group (2–3 minutes).

Why Understanding Ourselves Matters

When the gospel comes to us, it usually begins with a mirror. Wait . . . a mirror? You see, most people don't need to be convinced that the world just isn't the way it ought to be. But when you ask them why, they usually blame someone else: it is those bigots, or those liberals, or those conservatives, or those haters, or those . . . (on and on and on).

But the gospel doesn't start with *those* bad people *out there*. The gospel holds a mirror up to each one of us and forces us to reckon with what is actually true about *ourselves*. I am the bad guy (and so are you).

Through the passages you will read in a moment, God holds up a mirror to show us what is absolutely true about humanity—about us. Be prepared for a tough reality check. These verses are quite humbling.

But here's some encouragement: the bad news that you need to accept about yourself will make the good news of the gospel all the sweeter.

Reading

Read the Bible passages together (4–6 minutes).

As you read, think about these questions: What does this passage tell me about God? What does this passage tell me about humanity? You may wish to jot down some notes below.

- **Romans 1:18–25**

- **Romans 2:1–5**

- **Romans 3:9–20**

What do these passages tell me about God?

Notes:

What do these passages tell me about humanity?

Notes:

That we are bent toward
wickedness and even
tho we know God, we don't
glorify or give the thanks we
should.

4

ARTICLE

Read this article aloud as a group (9–12 minutes).

Paul had never met the people he was writing to in his letter to the Romans. These are some intense things to put in a letter to someone you've never met!

But as Paul sat down to write his letter to these Christians in Rome, he didn't want to assume anything about what they knew or didn't know about the gospel—so he started from the very beginning. Romans 1 teaches us that deep down, all people know some important things about God that are clear just from looking at creation (v. 20).

Paul wants us to know the truth about our Creator, but he also wants us to know the truth about ourselves. The first three chapters of Romans give us the opportunity to look into a mirror and see some stuff we wish was not there. We can learn three key things about people in these chapters.

HUMANITY IS INTENTIONALLY IGNORANT

As modern people, we feel insulted when we hear this. *You're saying I'm ignorant?!* However, Romans 1:18 tells us that the way we respond to what creation shows us about God is to deliberately "suppress the truth." Push it away. Pretend like it doesn't exist so we can live however we want.

Let's take a look at how and why this happens.

The Bible repeatedly tells us that creation's message about the Creator is clear. As Psalm 19:1 puts it, "The heavens declare the glory of God; the skies proclaim the work of his hands" (NIV). Creation tells us plainly that there is a higher power we have to answer to.

However, humans face two problems.

First, our knowledge of God is distorted because of sin. It is like we are looking through a broken lens. Though we can see something recognizable, it is impossible to get a clear picture.

Second, Romans 1 teaches us that because of sin, we actually *choose* to be ignorant. The truth that we *do* see, we suppress. Paul doesn't hold back in his description of people in Romans 1:19–21:

- They know the truth about God because he has made it obvious to them.
- Through everything God made, they can clearly see his eternal power and divine nature.
- So they have no excuse for not knowing God.

However . . .

- They wouldn't worship him as God or even give him thanks.
- They began to think up foolish ideas of what God was like.
- As a result, their minds became dark and confused.

We are all guilty of living as if God didn't exist. In our families, maybe we ignore or disrespect our parents. Maybe we envy our brothers and sisters—or maybe we put them down. As students, you have unique relationships and opportunities, but maybe you give your attention instead to things that just aren't important, wasting all kinds of time. Or maybe you make funny but hurtful comments about fellow students. These kinds of things make up a portrait of someone choosing to live in ignorance about God.

HUMANITY IS REBELLIOUS

Earlier we learned that the loving Creator-God is the supreme authority over all creation. What is humanity's response to his authority? Do we gladly honor him, believing that he is kind, generous, and worth obeying?

Not according to Romans 1.

Not only do we suppress truths God has directly revealed to us, but we also actively rebel against the things we know deep down he commands. Just as Adam and Eve rebelled against the one command God gave them, we rebel against the things we know in our gut we should obey.

Our rebellion starts with refusing to acknowledge that God is supreme. We don't treat God as honorable and magnificent. We refuse to give him thanks for giving us life and breath and everything else (Acts 17:25). Instead, we turn and worship almost everything but him.

There are two major ways humans can rebel, and they seem very different, but underneath they are similar.

For some of us, our rebellion takes the form of all kinds of sinful, harmful thoughts, words, and actions. A little further down in Romans 1, Paul presents a laundry list—sexual sin, greed, envy, quarrels, malice, gossip, and much more. We have all "been there" with these sins. Some of us are still there.

But others of us rebel against God in a different but equally foolish way: by living a life of self-righteousness. We might *look* good, but Paul says we are sinfully judgmental: "You may think you can condemn such people, but you are just as bad, and you have no excuse! When you say they are wicked and should be punished, you are condemning yourself, for you who judge others do these very same things" (Romans 2:1 NLT). Then Paul makes it 100 percent clear that we can't *earn* our way into God's favor by trying to be good: "For no one can ever be made right with God by doing what the law commands" (Romans 3:20 NLT). No amount of church attendance, good deeds, or moral behavior can make us need God's help less.

It may come as a surprise to you that there are two ways to be lost! And although they look different, they come from the same basic sin. As Timothy Keller puts it, "Sin is not just breaking the rules, it is putting yourself in the place of God as Savior, Lord, and Judge. . . . There are two ways to be your own Savior and Lord. One is breaking all the moral laws and setting your own course, and one is by keeping all the moral laws and being very, very good."[1]

The common thread in both kinds of rebellion is our prideful self-reliance. Standing firm before God's just judgment is only possible through repentance and accepting the righteousness that comes from Jesus.

HUMANITY IS CONDEMNED TO DEATH

What is the consequence of humanity's deliberate ignorance and rebellion? Judgment before God, the Judge. This is what we see in the opening pages of Genesis. God lavished his goodness on Adam and Eve, and he gave them just one command to obey. He warned them what the sentence would be if they disobeyed: "on the day you eat from [the tree], you will certainly die" (Genesis 2:17).

That death sentence now hangs over the head of every person. We have all have sinned and fall short of God's glory (Romans 3:23). We try to find excuses for our sin—and some of them seem like very good excuses—but somewhere, deep down, we know that we can't justify what we've done. One day, we will stand silent before the Judge and *know* that his sentence is just and true.

PUTTING IT ALL TOGETHER

Based on Romans 1–3, we can define our sin this way: my rejection of the knowledge of God and his authority over me as my Creator. This rejection is shown in my deliberate ignorance of him and my rebellion against his commands.

But you can ask God to help you see him and yourself honestly. And the truth doesn't need to scare us. God is "wonderfully kind, tolerant, and patient" (Romans 2:4 NLT). This Judge has chosen to offer us a way to stand in front of him on judgment day without fear. We can rest in the knowledge that God has provided a Savior. And we can reassure others of this truth as well.

Group members should take 5–6 minutes to look over the questions individually. Then the group should discuss the questions together (10 minutes).

1. Think about the big questions humans have asked themselves throughout history: *Why are we here? What is wrong with the world? What will put things right?* How did you answer these questions before you knew Christ? How do you answer them now?

2. In this week's article, we looked at three ways we can understand human sinfulness, based on our readings in Romans.

Fill in right side of the chart with these three aspects of sinfulness. Notice how they line up with the three aspects of God we discussed in session 2 and 3.

GOD		HUMANITY
Loving Creator	→	Rebellious
Supreme authority	→	_____
Final Judge	→	_____

3. What are the two different ways people rebel against God and go their own way?

a. _____

_____

What might this kind of rebellion look like in a person's life? Consider possible thoughts, attitudes, words, and actions.

b. _____

_____

What might this kind of rebellion look like in a person's life? Consider possible thoughts, attitudes, words, and actions.

4. Which of these two ways of sinning is more tempting for you?

Be alert this week for when you feel pulled one way or the other. Pray that our loving God would help you when you are tempted. And when you see that you have sinned, pray for forgiveness, knowing that when our hope is in Jesus, there is *no sin* that God will not forgive.

SURVEY

Survey two or three people by asking them the questions below. Before beginning your conversations, review "Tips for Conducting Your Surveys" (p. 4). You will share what you found out the next time your group meets.

Write the answers people give you in the spaces below.

Person #1

On a scale of one to ten, one being completely evil and ten being completely good, how would you rate people in general?

Why did you give people this rating?

Is there such a thing as "sin"? If so, what is it?

Person #2

On a scale of one to ten, one being completely evil and ten being completely good, how would you rate people in general?

Why did you give people this rating?

Is there such a thing as "sin"? If so, what is it?

Person #3

On a scale of one to ten, one being completely evil and ten being completely good, how would you rate people in general?

Why did you give people this rating?

Is there such a thing as "sin"? If so, what is it?

Notes for Yourself:

What did you learn from your survey?

What connections do you see between the survey responses and the article or Scriptures you've been studying?

SESSION

MEETING JESUS

SHARING TIME (*10 minutes*)

Have group members share what they learned from the surveys they conducted over the past week.

- Do you notice any common themes in what group members heard?
- What connections do you see between survey answers and what you are learning in this study?

INTRODUCTION

Read this introduction aloud as a group (2–3 minutes).

Jesus Is at the Center of the Gospel!

Almost anyone we're likely to meet has heard of Jesus **Christ**. But what do most people think of him? Many would say they admire Jesus. They might describe him as a great teacher, a peacemaker, or maybe even an example to follow.

Unfortunately, the view most people have of Jesus is different from who he really is.

So who *is* Jesus? Is he the tortured man suffering on a cross? Is he the dude in the long gown and glowing halo gently knocking on the door of your heart? Is he the revolutionary fighting the system? No wonder people are confused about the identity of Jesus Christ—there are a lot of versions of him floating around. We need to discover the real Jesus and let him speak for himself.

The Bible says a lot about Jesus. Here are some essential things to know. He is not just a wise person who lived a long time ago. He is God, so he has been around for eternity. All of creation was made through him (see John 1:3). He became human so that he could rescue us from our bondage to sin and our sentence of death. We're going to take a look at just how he did that.

Reading

Read the Bible passage together (4–6 minutes).

As you read, think about these questions: Based on this passage, what is the gospel message? What evidence does this passage offer to show that Jesus has been raised from the dead? As you read, you may wish to jot down some notes below.

- **1 Corinthians 15:1–8, 12–26**

Based on this passage, what is the gospel message?

Notes:

What evidence does this passage offer to show that Jesus has been raised from the dead?

Notes:

ARTICLE

Read this article aloud as a group (9–12 minutes).

CHRIST: PERFECTLY OBEDIENT

Every birth is extraordinary, of course. A tiny new human makes a dramatic entrance into the world!

Jesus's birth took *extraordinary* to a new level: the guiding star, multitudes of angels in the night sky, wise men journeying from afar. But after all that, Jesus spent the next nearly thirty years living a pretty low-key life in a pretty unexciting place, learning a trade, eventually earning a living with his hands, and going to synagogue on Saturdays.

That changed when Jesus was about thirty years old. Then we see him in the Jordan River being baptized. At this incredible moment, God the Father proclaims from heaven, "This is my Son!" and the **Holy Spirit** descends on Jesus in the form of a dove.

What is going on in this scene? The Hero-King of the Big Gospel Story is finally being revealed and given God's seal of approval. Just as officers are commissioned when they join the military, Jesus is being commissioned in his baptism to do the saving work he came for. Finally, the rescue plan to save fallen people was underway!

But then . . . **the devil** crashes the scene.

Jesus, led by the Holy Spirit, goes out into the wilderness, where he **fasts** for forty days and nights. After Jesus has gone for so long without food, he is hungry and weak. It is then that the devil approaches him. Satan's goal is to stop Jesus's rescue mission before it can start. His strategy is to put a wedge between Jesus and God (as he had done with Adam and Eve), getting Jesus to distrust God, to take shortcuts in his mission, and to win power and wealth for himself by siding with Satan.

The devil is crafty. He tries to use Jesus's hunger against him, and he twists Scripture verses to try to deceive Jesus into doing what he wants him to do.

Satan attacks Jesus three times, each time with a slightly different strategy. Every time, Jesus quotes Scripture, using its truth to defend himself against the devil's lies. Defeated, the devil leaves. (For the full story, see Matthew 4:1–11.)

Now let's put this scene together with what you already know. The appearance of Satan here is a clue to stop and remember the garden of Eden in Genesis. There, in his curse, God promised that the future offspring of Eve would crush Satan's head. Now, as Jesus is being baptized in the Jordan River, it is as if God is announcing that the Snake Crusher has arrived—and the devil is desperate to stop him.

There are some remarkable similarities between Jesus's temptation and that of Adam and Eve. In both, Satan offers food as a temptation. In both, Satan twists God's words to introduce doubt. And in both, Satan promises you can be like God.

Yet there are also major differences. In the garden, there was food *everywhere*. Adam and Eve could have anything they wanted except for the fruit of one tree. In the desert, there is nothing—and Jesus is very hungry. It's like Jesus is in a boxing ring blindfolded and with his hands tied behind his back.

Most importantly, this desert meet-up is a complete reversal of the disaster in the garden. Even with all the odds in their favor, Adam and Eve just handed their God-given authority over to Satan at the first sign of temptation. But in the desert, Jesus stays strong against Satan, even when his body is weak. He defends God, untwisting Satan's misuse of Scripture and launching the truth right back in his face. Jesus overcomes the first hurdle in accomplishing his mission.

As God's Son, Jesus did not inherit the curse of sin, and he's not about to choose that miserable path himself, even if it looks like a major shortcut. Jesus remains sinless, and this desert scene is just one snapshot from an entire life lived in perfect obedience to his Father. As we read the Bible, we see that Jesus's obedience means more than just avoiding bad things. Jesus lives a perfectly obedient life that mirrors God's goodness: he reaches out to the needy; he feeds the hungry; he heals; he teaches; he welcomes. In short, he loves.

CHRIST: WILLING TO DIE IN OUR PLACE

What does Christ's perfect obedience actually mean for us? Should we look at him and admire his abilities? Is he just a good example for us to follow?

If that were all there is to Jesus, we would still be stuck without a solution to our sin problem. Even if Jesus is perfectly good, we're still stuck in our own rebelliousness. We still defy God's authority. A inspiring role model is not enough.

Maybe you've read or seen *The Lion, the Witch, and the Wardrobe*. In it, Edmund betrays the rightful king, Aslan the lion. The Witch who has stolen the throne is keeping Edmund captive. She declares that, according to the laws of the land, because Edmund is a traitor, he must die. And she's right.

Sinful humans are like Edmund. They've sinned against the true King and have put themselves under the power of death and Satan, the rebel who tried to steal the throne of the King.

When God gave humans the death sentence for their rebellion, he was being completely just. If God had required anything less than perfect obedience, it would have been saying that sin was not all that bad. But we can see for ourselves the effects of sin, from conflict within families to large-scale war and destruction. Not punishing sin would have been an injustice.

In other words . . . we were in a hopeless situation that no role model could have gotten us out of.

But Jesus is far more than a good example! Here's one way to sum up what Jesus's rescue mission achieved: "[God] made the one who did not know sin [that is, Jesus] to be sin for us, so that in him we might become the righteousness of God" (2 Corinthians 5:21). Another way of putting it: "God made Christ, who never sinned, to be the offering for our sin, so that we could be made right with God through Christ" (NLT).

This verse sums up what is sometimes called the Great Exchange. We're familiar with exchanging gifts: you give someone a present, and they give you one in return. Now, in the Great Exchange, what does Jesus give those who believe in him? And what do they give him? Jesus gives his righteousness, his life of perfect obedience. He earned a grade of 100 percent in the course of life—where 100 percent is passing and anything else is failing. That is what Jesus gives us. And what does he get from us? Our sin. Our failing grade.

We've already seen the description of people in the first book of Romans: not good.

But Jesus says he's like a shepherd who comes to rescue helpless sheep: "I am the good shepherd. The good shepherd lays down his life for the sheep . . . . I lay down my life for the sheep. . . . No one takes it from me, but I lay it down on my own" (John 10:11, 15, 18).

Jesus Christ volunteered to take on people's sin—this darkness that has caused murder and depression and evil—this sin that is to blame for every tear ever cried. Jesus became *this* sin for us. He gave himself to be killed on the cross, taking the punishment we had earned.

CHRIST: VICTORIOUS OVER DEATH

Yet if everything Jesus did ended with his death, how terrible that would be!

It wasn't enough for Jesus to experience death; he had to *defeat* it so that it couldn't come for us. If Jesus hadn't defeated it, Satan would still be threatening us with never-ending death.

God raised Jesus from the dead, and in his resurrection, Jesus gained the victory over death. God the Just brought Jesus the Sinless One back to life.

That's great news for us! Romans 6:4–5 tells us, "For we died and were buried with Christ by baptism. And just as Christ was raised from the dead by the glorious power of the Father, now we also may live new lives. Since we have been united with him in his death, we will also be raised to life as he was" (NLT).

The victorious resurrection of Christ guarantees our future victory over the grave. We will die; but if we have trusted that Jesus paid for our sin, we will be raised, as Jesus was, to life without end.

GOD		HUMANITY		CHRIST
Loving Creator	→	Intentionally ignorant	→	Perfectly obedient
Supreme authority	→	Rebellious	→	Willing to die in our place
Final Judge	→	Condemned to death	→	Victorious over death

But that's not all Jesus's resurrection achieves. People who follow Christ can live a new life here on earth. Romans 6 teaches us that we can say *no* to sin and *yes* to righteousness. We are no longer in slavery to sin! Colossians 3 teaches us how to "put off" our old way of life and "put on" things like compassion, kindness, and humility.

This is huge! Our sin condemned us to death, but Christ took our punishment and rose victorious. And that victory is ours to live in every single day, until we too are raised in victory over the grave. Jesus is truly the offspring from Eve that crushed Satan and brought us freedom!

WORDS TO KNOW

Christ: The long-awaited Messiah, the Anointed One who will save the world from sin. He is the One who was first hinted at in Genesis 3:15. That reference begins a long series of biblical "arrows" pointing to Jesus (who is called the "Christ" more than five hundred times in the New Testament).

Holy Spirit: God is a Trinity—he is Three-in-One. The Father, the Son (Jesus), and the Holy Spirit are the three Persons that make up the one God. In the Old Testament, God filled only certain special people with his Holy Spirit. In the New Testament, after Jesus rises from the dead and ascends into heaven, the Holy Spirit fills everyone who comes to Christ in faith.

The devil: Another way to refer to Satan, who is also known as the accuser. He is a spirit who works against God and against God's people. Jesus has already defeated him by resisting all his temptations, living a perfect life, and then dying and rising to rescue his people. In the final days, the devil will be "thrown into the lake of fire" (Revelation 20:10).

Fast: To go without eating and sometimes also drinking. After being baptized by John the Baptist and before being tempted by the devil, Jesus fasted in the wilderness for "forty days and forty nights" (Matthew 4:2). After withstanding Satan's attempts at leading him astray, Jesus was ready to begin his ministry.

DISCUSSION

Group members should take 5–6 minutes to look over the questions individually. Then the group should discuss the questions together (10 minutes).

1. Complete the chart.

GOD		HUMANITY		CHRIST
Loving Creator	→	Intentionally ignorant	→	_____ _____
Supreme authority	→	Rebellious	→	_____ _____
Final Judge	→	Condemned to death	→	_____ _____

2. How is the temptation of Jesus different from the temptation of Adam and Eve?

Why is this important?

3. What do we get from Jesus in the Great Exchange that happened when he died on the cross?

4. Why is the resurrection of Jesus Christ so important for Christians?

5. How does being united with the risen Christ change your everyday life?

SURVEY

Survey two or three people by asking them the question below. Before beginning your conversations, review "Tips for Conducting Your Surveys" (p. 4). You will share what you found out the next time your group meets.

Write the answers people give you in the spaces below.

This week's question is: *Who is Jesus?*

Remember to be a LISTENER.

Some might say Jesus is their Lord and Savior. If they do, you can ask them, *How would your life be different if Christ were not a part of it?*

Some might say Jesus was a historical figure but is not the Son of God. Or they might say Jesus may be the answer for some people but not for them. If so, you can ask them, *Why do you believe this? What led you to this view?* Depending on how the conversation is going, you might be able to share what you have learned about God and humanity. If they are not interested in hearing what you've learned, then don't share. Keep it friendly!

Person #1

Who is Jesus?

Person #2

Who is Jesus?

Person #3

Who is Jesus?

Notes for Yourself:

What did you learn from your survey?

What connections do you see between the survey responses and the article or Scriptures you've been studying?

BEING MADE RIGHT WITH GOD

SHARING TIME (*10 minutes*)

Have group members share what they learned from the surveys they conducted over the past week.

- Do you notice any common themes in what group members heard?
- What connections do you see between survey answers and what you are learning in this study?

INTRODUCTION

Read this introduction aloud as a group (2–3 minutes).

Why Justification Matters

Justification is at the heart of the gospel, so it's important for us to understand it.

Justification means we are made right in God's eyes. We are justified, declared **righteous**. Our sin has been dealt with, and instead having a failing record of sin, we have Jesus's perfect record of righteousness.

A lot of people don't understand this very important part of Christianity.

Some people think Christians claim to be better than other people. But in fact, Christ-followers claim zero credit for being right in God's eyes. Everything they have is a gift—so Christians should actually be the humblest people on the planet!

Some Christians get confused too. They feel burdened by trying to be good enough for God. They live under a cloud of guilt and shame—a miserable way to walk through life! But this is *not* the kind of life Jesus saved us for. We are justified by what Jesus has done, and that justification frees us from guilt and shame.

As you dive into these readings, ask God to open your eyes to take in the freedom of justification.

Reading

Read the Bible passages together (4–6 minutes).

As you read, notice how often the following terms appear: **grace**, **faith** (or **believing**), and **righteous** (or **righteousness**). You may wish to jot down some notes on these ideas below.

(Note: The readings also frequently mention the **law**. To read about the law, see "Words to Know.")

- **Romans 3:20–28**

- **Romans 4:1–5, 18–25**

Grace

Notes:

Faith

Notes:

Righteous

Notes:

ARTICLE

Read this article aloud as a group (9–12 minutes).

The word *justification* hardly ever comes up in conversation. When it does, it's often negative: "What possible justification can they give for that terrible behavior?" When we say we're trying to justify our actions, there's a good chance we're just trying to get out of trouble: "He came up with every excuse in the book to justify all the rude things he said."

In contrast, the justification we find in the Bible is rich and true and life-giving. It means no longer being guilty in God's eyes and no longer deserving punishment. It means being made righteous and receiving new life.

Let's focus on a few things our reading in Romans says about justification.

1. "No one will be justified in his sight by the works of the law" (Romans 3:20). We have all failed. None of us can ever earn a perfect record.

2. "But now, apart from the law, the righteousness of God has been revealed" (v. 21). *But now.* Those words announce a 180-degree turnaround! *But now* God steps in. He himself provides a righteousness that has nothing to do with using good works to earn it. He makes everyone who believes in Jesus righteous.

3. "They are justified freely by his grace" (v. 24). God declares us innocent even though we don't deserve it. We don't earn righteousness; God gives it to us.

4. "A person is justified by faith" (v. 28). Paul repeats this super-important point: We receive justification by faith, *not* by good works

we do. Jesus does the justifying. Jesus gives us his righteousness. All we do is receive it as we trust him.

Based on these truths from the Bible, we can define justification this way: God, out of his love and grace, takes away the record of all our sins. In its place, he gives us the record of perfect righteousness that Jesus earned. Our sins are forgiven, removed completely. According to God, we are now righteous.

That's the nutshell version. But there's much more to discover!

JUSTIFICATION: WE ARE MORE THAN JUST INNOCENT

Imagine this: you're standing in front of a judge, waiting to be sentenced for a crime you committed. The verdict comes in: *Guilty!* The sentence comes in: *Death!* Your heart sinks. But then something shocking happens. The judge gets up, walks over to where you are seated, and tells the guard to release you. As you stand free, you see the judge himself being placed in your chains, taking your punishment. You are set free because the judge became your substitute.

This would be mind-blowing enough—yet justification is much better still!

For this story to be like the justification God provides, the judge would then have to hand you his wallet and keys, saying, "I give you everything I own. My car, my house, my bank account—it's all yours."

This is justification. Jesus took the punishment for our sin when he died on the cross, AND God gives you all the righteousness and perfection of Jesus! That's the Great Exchange we talked a little bit about in our last lesson.

One of my favorite Christian writers, R. C. Sproul, created a great picture to illustrate justification: the three circles.[2]

Here's what to do with the three circles you see below:

- Color in the circle on the left completely. This is a picture of us in our guilt. We are full of darkness and death and sin.
- Leave the middle circle totally empty. This shows the first part of justification: our sin is taken away and we are declared innocent.
- Fill the circle on the right with plus signs—lots of plus signs! This shows the second part of justification: not only has our sin been removed, but we have received the righteousness of Jesus.

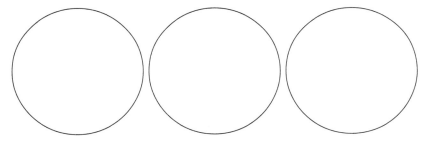

HOW DO WE RECEIVE JUSTIFICATION?

God declares us innocent and Christ gives us his righteousness. That's an amazingly good deal! How do we get it? The Bible's answer is clear: by faith alone.

> Because we know that a person is not justified by the works of the law but by faith in Jesus Christ, even we ourselves have believed in Christ Jesus. This was so that we might be justified by faith in Christ and not by the works of the law, because by the works of the law no human being will be justified. (Galatians 2:16)

> For you are saved by grace through faith, and this is not from yourselves; it is God's gift—not from works, so that no one can boast. (Ephesians 2:8–9)

Justification comes by God's *grace*—it's a free gift that we don't deserve and could never earn. Justification also comes to us by *faith*, which means we trust God to do this amazing thing we could never do for ourselves.

JUSTIFICATION IN ACTION: A STORY

I've said a lot about justification. But sometimes a story is the best way to drive the point home.

The **Merciful** King[3]

Once upon a time, there lived a great king. He was the most powerful man in the kingdom, but he was also the kindest and gentlest. The kingdom was known for its peace and harmony. Years would go by without a single crime being committed.

One day, however, the king's chief servant entered the throne room with bad news. "There is a thief in the realm, sire," said the servant. The king was astonished! "Find that thief! And when you do, bring him to me. He will be punished with ten lashes!" Everyone was astonished. It had been so long since a crime had been committed that they couldn't imagine who would have done such a thing.

A week went by, and the servant again entered the throne room. "I have bad news, sire," the servant reported quietly. "The thief has not been found. He continues to steal from your people." In anger, the king raised his voice and said, "Find the thief, and when you do, he will receive twenty-five lashes!" The people began to murmur, "Who could possibly be committing such a crime? And who could bear such a punishment?"

After a time, the servant reappeared. "Your Majesty, we have searched in vain for the thief. Your people are still being robbed." The king was enraged. "Find that wretched thief!

And when you do, the punishment will be fifty lashes!" Now the people were filled with dread. They weren't even sure the king himself could survive such a punishment. And if he could not, then no one could.

Soon afterward, the servant once again approached the king. His face was pale and his voice timid. "Your Highness, the thief has been found."

"Bring him to me this instant!" cried the king. The crowd that had poured into the throne room slowly parted, revealing the trembling thief. To the utter shock and dismay of all, it was the king's elderly mother.

There she stood, crying, her frail body shaking with fear and shame. She was the very last soul that anyone would have suspected. And there stood the king, deeply wounded. The crowd began to wonder, *What will the merciful king do? Will he set aside the law and show his love and mercy by forgiving his mother for her crimes? Or will he display his authority and justice by giving her exactly what she deserves? Will he choose mercy or will he choose justice?*

"Bring the whipping post!" commanded the king. The crowd was stunned. Would the king truly give his mother fifty lashes? Even the king could scarcely survive such a flogging! The old woman was tied to the post. Her dress was torn to expose her back to the whipmaster. She was so thin and weak that her ribs could be counted. "Begin the whipping!" said the king.

The whip was raised.

But just as the whipmaster was about to unleash his first stroke, the king cried, "Halt!" The crowd sighed in relief. But not for long. The king rose from his throne. He removed the crown from his head. As he walked toward his mother, he laid aside his royal robe. When he reached his mother, he wrapped his strong body around her, shielding her completely. "Now, begin the whipping," said the king.

In this story, the king displays pure mercy and perfect justice, like our King who is both "just and the one who justifies those who have faith in Jesus" (Romans 3:26 NIV).

THE TAKEAWAY

I hope that reading about what Jesus has done for you in justification has moved you to love God more!

But what does it mean in our daily lives?

First, understanding justification should lift the burden of feeling like you need to do good things so that you'll be accepted by God. We cannot earn God's acceptance by things we do. We all sin. It is impossible for us to get our own perfect record. Trying to earn God's acceptance by trying hard to do lots of good things will wear us out and frustrate us. Paul writes, "It is for freedom that Christ has set us free" (Galatians 5:1 NIV). Accept the freedom of God's freely offered justification! Remind yourself of it daily.

Similarly, once we have accepted the gift of justification, there's nothing we can do to make God love us more! We are already God's "dearly loved children" (Ephesians 5:1). Rest in the security of that love.

Second, understanding justification should lift the burden of guilt you feel over your sins. Being justified doesn't mean that you suddenly become sinless. Jesus died for the sins you commit as a believer just as much as he died for the sins you committed before you believed. Seek forgiveness, and let Jesus lift the guilt from your shoulders.

Finally, understanding justification will help you as you speak with others about Jesus. There are many misunderstandings out there about how to become acceptable to God. You can help bring clarity and truth—and freedom!

WORDS TO KNOW

Righteous: Good; pleasing to God; blameless.

Grace: A free, undeserved gift from God. God gives us his love and salvation—and Jesus's perfect righteousness—even though we don't deserve any of it.

Faith: Having faith in Jesus means *believing* that he is who he says he is (the Son of God) and *trusting* that what he has done for us through his death and resurrection is completely effective in saving us.

Law: The *law* is made up of the many commandments God gave his people in the Old Testament. The most famous of these are the Ten Commandments, but there were hundreds more. The law showed the ancient Israelites how to live as God's people, including what they could eat and how they were to worship God. The law reflects God's perfect holiness. No human but Jesus could *ever* keep the law perfectly, so no person would ever be able to earn a perfect record before God. But the law helps us see that we fall short of God's perfect standard.

Merciful: Full of mercy. Here, *mercy* means not giving someone the bad consequences they deserve. The king in this story is merciful because he takes the punishment the thief deserved. God is merciful because in Christ he takes the punishment we deserved.

DISCUSSION

Group members should take 5–6 minutes to look over the questions individually. Then the group should discuss the questions together (10 minutes).

1. In your own words, explain what justification is.

2. "We are more than just innocent." What does this statement mean, and why is it important? (Remember the story about the judge.)

3. How do we receive justification?

4. How should the truth about justification change our lives?

5. How do you think understanding justification can help you as you share the gospel with others?

SURVEY

Survey two or three people by asking them the question below. Before beginning your conversations, review "Tips for Conducting Your Surveys" (p. 4). You will share what you found out the next time your group meets.

Write the answers people give you in the spaces below.

This week's question is: *Is there more than one way to God? Please explain.* In the biblical view, Christ is the way, the truth, and the life, and no one comes to the Father except through him (John 14:6). However, many believe there are multiple ways to God.

Your first task, as usual, will be to LISTEN. It is fascinating to learn what people believe about this question. And try to understand *why* they believe what they do. What has influenced their beliefs?

Person #1

Is there more than one way to God? Please explain.

Person #2

Is there more than one way to God? Please explain.

Person #3

Is there more than one way to God? Please explain.

Notes for Yourself:

What did you learn from your survey?

What connections do you see between the survey responses and the article or the Scriptures about justification you've been studying?

RESPONDING TO THE GOSPEL

INTRODUCTION

Read this introduction aloud as a group (2–3 minutes).

Why Our Response Matters

So far in our study, we've mainly focused on what the gospel message *is*. But we also need to talk about how to respond to it. In the Bible, we see examples of people understanding the gospel and then responding by repenting, believing, and getting baptized.

Consider your own life for a moment. Think of the most hurtful sin you've ever committed. It's painful to think about, isn't it?

Real Christians don't pretend to be sinless. In fact, as Christians, we are more aware of our sins than we ever were before. The difference is that we know what to do with our sin. The gospel teaches us how to repent and be freed from it so that we're not haunted and weighed down by guilt.

This is what's so amazing about the gospel. By repenting, you can turn away from your sin and be a new person. Faith in Jesus means your sin is forgiven forever. What joy to leave your sin and shame behind!

That sin you thought of? Jesus isn't shocked by it. He already died for it. Let him take it away!

Responding to the gospel message in faith is freeing!

Reading

Read the Bible passage together (4–6 minutes).

Background: You might know that the ancient Greeks were famous for their philosophers. This passage mentions two groups of philosophers that were in the audience listening to Paul: the *Epicureans* and the *Stoics*. These two groups believed different things, but they had at least two things in common: they did not believe in a single personal God like the God of the Bible, and they loved to debate. Paul knows his audience and chooses his words carefully. The *Areopagus* was "Athens's chief court, consisting . . . of probably roughly a hundred elite members. They had authority to evaluate new cults [or religions] coming to town."[4]

In the little sermon in this week's passage, Paul touches on some of the key themes of the gospel that we have covered. As you read, notice what he says about *God* and *humanity* and *Jesus*. You may wish to jot down some notes below.

- Acts 17:16–34

God

Notes:

Humanity

Notes:

Jesus

Notes:

7

ARTICLE

Read this article aloud as a group (9–12 minutes).

If someone asked you, "What is the gospel?" you could answer by explaining justification and you would be spot-on. Justification is at the heart of what God has done for us in Christ.

But how does this truth apply to our lives?

Think of it like this. If you are asked, "How can I get rid of this headache?" there are two different ways of answering, and both of them are correct. You could explain what happens chemically inside the human body when a person takes pain medicine. Or you could say, "Here, swallow this pill, and your headache will go away." The first answer focuses on how the medicine works. The second answer tells you what to do.

We want people to understand what God has done for us in Christ—how the gospel works. We also want people to do something—to *respond*.

In this lesson, we'll explore how to respond to the gospel. We'll do that by listening in as Paul proclaims the gospel message and urges the people listening to respond.

Notice that in his visit to Athens, Paul has been "telling the good news about Jesus and the resurrection" (Acts 17:18) to pretty much anyone who will listen. As we've seen, the phrase *the good news* is another way of saying *the gospel*. The big thinkers of Athens have heard a little bit of Paul's news and want to hear more. They shove Paul up on center stage, put a mic in his hand, and sit down to listen.

From the Areopagus in Athens, Paul would have been able to see several impressive temples. These people were indeed "extremely religious" (Acts 17:22)—as are many modern-day people in many big cities and small villages around the world.

Paul seems to follow the script of Genesis 1–3 as he unpacks the gospel for that religious crowd. Paul describes a loving Creator who has supreme authority and is the final Judge. The descriptions of humanity and the descriptions of God are as true today as they were on that ancient hill in Athens.

And just as Paul gets to the high point of his presentation—the resurrection of Jesus—some of the people in the crowd begin to make fun of him, and his audience breaks up for the day. But even though we don't have the last page of Paul's sermon notes, we can see where he was going and we can see the response he was calling for. The Creator and Judge of all the earth commands every person on his earth to repent (Acts 17:30).

What does it mean to repent? John Stott states, "Repentance is a definite turn from every thought, word, deed and habit which is known to be wrong. . . . It is an inward change of mind and attitude toward sin which leads to a change of behavior."[5] When we repent, we turn around. We turn *away from wrong things* that we've done or said or thought, and *away from our failure* to do or say or think good things. We then turn *toward God* in faith, asking his forgiveness and his help as we genuinely seek change in our lives.

The command to repent and believe can be found as early as the very first sermon Jesus gave: "Jesus went to Galilee, proclaiming the good news of God: 'The time is fulfilled, and the kingdom of God has come near. Repent and believe the good news!'" (Mark 1:14–15).

Repentance and belief go together like inhaling and exhaling. Both are essential to the Christian life. Repentance describes what we turn from, and belief describes what we turn toward. In repentance, we change our minds about sin and reject it. In belief, we trust in the finished work of Jesus for the forgiveness of sins and the hope of eternal life. Again, this gospel is not just information. It's not just a story. The gospel impacts reality! Through repentance and belief, the good news is actually applied to our lives.

The call to people everywhere is the same now as it was then: repent and believe.

BAPTISM

In the New Testament, there was a physical part of responding to the gospel message in faith: people who repented and believed were baptized to show outwardly that something had changed inwardly.

Look at what the apostle Paul says about baptism:

> Or have you forgotten that when we were joined with Christ Jesus in baptism, we joined him in his death? For we died and were buried with Christ by baptism. And just as Christ was raised from the dead by the glorious power of the Father, now we also may live new lives. (Romans 6:3–4 NLT)

> For you were buried with Christ when you were baptized. And with him you were raised to new life because you trusted the mighty power of God, who raised Christ from the dead. You were dead because of your sins and because your sinful nature was not yet cut away. Then God made you alive with Christ, for he forgave all our sins. (Colossians 2:12–13 NLT)

Baptism shows that someone has embraced the gospel of Jesus Christ and become united with him. It is why Jesus commanded his followers, "All authority has been given to me in heaven and on earth. Go, therefore, and make disciples of all nations, *baptizing them in the name of the Father and of the Son and of the Holy Spirit*, teaching them to observe everything I have commanded you. And remember,

I am with you always, to the end of the age" (Matthew 28:18–20, emphasis added).

The core content of the gospel is justification. It is how God makes us right with him. The core response to the gospel is repenting and believing. And the outward sign of this inner change is baptism.

THE TAKEAWAY

As we discussed in previous sessions, people do not want to admit they are not in control of their own destiny. We are naturally ignorant and rebellious. However, this is precisely why repentance and belief are such powerful gifts: they go against our natural tendencies. And while rebellion brought death, repentance and faith bring true life.

Repentance is like refreshing rain: "Therefore repent and turn back, so that your sins may be wiped out, that seasons of refreshing may come from the presence of the Lord" (Acts 3:19–20).

Repentance brings a clean conscience: "For godly grief produces a repentance that leads to salvation without regret" (2 Corinthians 7:10).

Baptism shows the move from death to life. And in our new life, we are brought back into God's beautiful kingdom of things as they should be. We can breathe again! We are free!

As you seek to connect this lesson with your life, you can think about who in your life is in need of the refreshing that only comes through repentance. Perhaps you yourself need to ask God to give you the refreshing gifts of repentance and belief. Or maybe your next step is to be baptized or to encourage a new believer to be baptized.

DISCUSSION

Group members should take 5–6 minutes to look over the questions individually. Then the group should discuss the questions together (10 minutes).

1. Acts 17 shows us how Paul studied the culture of the ancient Greeks of Athens. He looked at their statues and quoted their poetry, trying to connect with the people he was speaking to. What do you find particularly helpful about Paul's example of how to talk with others about the gospel?

2. What is repentance? What is belief? What is the connection between repentance and belief?

3. What is baptism a picture of?

4. Take a few moments on your own to reflect on these two questions:

How did you respond to the gospel the first time you heard it?

What do repentance and belief look like in your own life?

SURVEY

Survey two or three people by asking them the question below. Before beginning your conversations, review "Tips for Conducting Your Surveys" (p. 4). You will share what you found out the next time your group meets.

Write the answers people give you in the spaces below.

This week's question is: *How will God decide who goes to heaven and who goes to hell?*

Some things to listen for: As people answer this question, you will hear their view of God, heaven, hell, faith and works, and justification. No matter what their thoughts are, LISTEN carefully so that you really understand what they are saying. *If* the person you are surveying is open to it, you *might* have an opportunity to share your own view—but the most important thing is to hear the other person out.

Here are some views that you might hear:

Some people have a "balance" view: if you do more good than bad, you'll go to heaven, but if you do more bad than good, you'll go to hell. In this case, remember what you've learned so far about humankind: all fall short of the glory of God.

Others will lean into only one part of God's character: God is love, so surely no one will go to hell. In this case, consider what you've learned about the fullness of God's character. He is loving. But he is also just. Sin cannot go unpunished.

Still others will view both heaven and hell as made-up ideas. In this case, consider what we learned early on about how human beings suppress or ignore the truth. Maybe the person you're talking to would be willing to share *why* they believe these are made-up ideas. What led them to this belief?

Person #1:

How will God decide who goes to heaven and who goes to hell?

Person #2:

How will God decide who goes to heaven and who goes to hell?

Person #3:

How will God decide who goes to heaven and who goes to hell?

Notes for Yourself

What did you learn from your survey? What connections do you see between the survey responses and the article or the Scriptures you've been studying?

SESSION

GROWING AND CHANGING

SHARING TIME (*10 minutes*)

> ## SHARING TIME (*10 minutes*)
>
> Have group members share what they learned from the surveys they conducted over the past week.
> - Do you notice any common themes in what group members heard?
> - What connections do you see between survey answers and what you are learning in this study?

INTRODUCTION

Read this introduction aloud as a group (2–3 minutes).

Why Change Matters

Once we respond to the gospel with repentance and faith, we're not immediately made perfect and taken up into heaven. Instead, we walk back into the same old, hard world. But something *has* changed: we have a new life. We belong to God, and we are being transformed to be more like Jesus.

While we are not perfect, we no longer need to live in shame because of our failures. Instead, when we confess our sins to God, we receive forgiveness and hope for lasting change. And because God places his

Holy Spirit in everyone he has justified through Jesus, there's a whole new power at work inside of us to bring good growth into our lives.

We belong to Christ! He is changing everything—and he won't stop until he comes again, when we will be fully restored images of God, perfectly reflecting his love and holiness.

Reading

Read the Bible passages together (4–6 minutes).

As you read each passage, think about the main point Paul is making. You may want to jot down some notes below.

- **Romans 6:5–14**

- **Romans 8:1–16**

- **Romans 8:33–39**

- **Romans 12:1–2**

8

ARTICLE

Read this article aloud as a group (9–12 minutes).

A NEW LIFE AND A NEW IDENTITY

When you were young, you might have read some fairy tales. If you did, you know that a lot of them end with words like "They lived happily ever after." Apparently, Cinderella and Snow White and Sleeping Beauty get a *new* life in which they never have to face anything like *real* life.

Now, happy endings can be fun. Not everything we read or watch has to be heavy. The more you grow up, the more you realize that real life is more complicated than a fairy tale.

The gospel, though it takes the form of a story you can read in the Bible, is *not* a fairy tale.

Once we have responded to Jesus in faith, we are given a new life. But it's not a life in a problem-free bubble, magically cut off from the hard things in the real world. And it's not a life that's free of sin.

In describing the Christian life, many believers speak of the *already* and the *not yet*. The *already* refers to all the blessings we experience now in Christ. The *not yet* refers to the blessings we will experience in the future, after we have died and been raised and after Jesus returns and establishes the new heaven and the new earth.

In previous sessions, we have seen some of the *already* blessings that are ours when we believe in Jesus: being justified, having our sins taken care of, experiencing new freedom. And this week we see a few more:

the Holy Spirit, a new identity as children of God, and a promise that nothing "will be able to separate us from the love of God that is in Christ Jesus our Lord" (Romans 8:39).

Our new life won't be perfect. But with all of these blessings, it will certainly look different from our old life. God doesn't expect instant transformation, but he does call us to begin to live out our new identity as his children. Romans 12:2—"Do not be conformed to this age, but be transformed by the renewing of your mind, so that you may discern what is the good, pleasing, and perfect will of God"—is an ongoing reality. The renewing of our mind isn't something that already happened and is finished, but it is *happening*—a continuing process as we live our new life in Christ.

SANCTIFICATION

This growth—the transforming and renewing of our minds and lives—is called sanctification. It is the process that makes us more and more like Jesus, and it is powered by the Holy Spirit in us.

Again, this is different from justification. Justification happens all at once: God declares that a believer is righteous because of Jesus. Done.

Sanctification is a lifelong process. This is important to note because all believers experience a tension in their life in Christ: if I have been given a new life and identity, why do I still sin? Paul takes some time to address this hard question. In Romans 6, Paul reassures us that when we have been united with Jesus by faith, we leave the old, sinful life behind:

> We know that our old sinful selves were crucified with Christ so that sin might lose its power in our lives. We are no longer slaves to sin. For when we died with Christ we were set free from the power of sin. (Romans 6:6–7 NLT)

The news that we aren't in slavery to sin anymore is huge. We don't *have* to do the sinful things we are tempted to do. So why do we still do them?

Because, as Paul writes in Romans 7, for as long as we are living in our bodies on earth, we will still have the "flesh" or "sinful nature" inside us (v. 18). This part of us still pulls us in the direction of sin, and it's why Paul speaks of a "war" that is being fought inside of him (v. 23). Here is how he describes his struggle:

> [W]hat I want to do I do not do, but what I hate I do. . . . As it is, it is no longer I myself who do it, but it is sin living in me. For I know that good itself does not dwell in me, that is, in my sinful nature [or "flesh"]. For I have the desire to do what is good, but I cannot carry it out. For I do not do the good I want to do, but the evil I do not want to do—this I keep on doing. (Romans 7:15, 17–19 NIV)

This sounds hard, doesn't it? Did getting a new life really change anything?

Yes!

Our first piece of encouraging news is that *nothing*, "neither death nor life, neither angels nor demons, neither the present nor the future, nor any powers, neither height nor depth, nor anything else in all creation, will be able to separate us from the love of God that is in Christ Jesus our Lord" (Romans 8:38–39 NIV). We are secure in our relationship with God!

The second encouragement is that God gives us the gift of the Holy Spirit. He isn't looking down on us and simply ordering us to clean up our lives. He knows that by ourselves, we wouldn't be able to accomplish lasting change. But his Spirit lives in us and makes change happen.

The Bible does give us commands—things to do and things not to do. As we just read, "*Do not let sin control* the way you live; *do not give in* to sinful desires. *Do not let* any part of your body become an instrument of evil to serve sin. Instead, *give yourselves* completely to God, for you were dead, but now you have new life" (Romans 6:12–13 NLT, emphasis added).

So we are called to act.

Yet God knows our weakness. And he reassures us that his power is with us, helping us, through his Holy Spirit. Romans 8:13, for example, says that we are to "put to death the deeds of [our] sinful nature" (NLT). But it also makes it clear that we don't do this on our own; we do it "through the power of the Spirit" (NLT). Paul's letter to the Philippians describes how God helps us as we seek to live Christlike lives: "Work hard to show the results of your salvation, obeying God with deep reverence and fear. For God is working in you, giving you the desire and the power to do what pleases him" (Philippians 2:12–13 NLT).

So God doesn't save us and then throw us into the deep end of the pool to sink or swim on our own. He is always with us by his Spirit, pouring supernatural power into our lives.

A final piece of encouragement is this: God has given us his Word so that one day the process of sanctification will be complete, and we will stand before him perfectly holy. Right now, in this life and in this world, that perfect holiness is part of the *not yet*. But we can count on God's promise that, on the last day, he will finish the work he has begun in us:

> Now may the God of peace himself sanctify you completely. And may your whole spirit, soul, and body be kept sound and blameless at the coming of our Lord Jesus Christ. He who calls you is faithful; he will do it. (1 Thessalonians 5:23–24)

What an encouragement!

ADOPTION

One of the most beautiful things in Romans is the news that we have been adopted into God's family. The Holy Spirit delivers us from slavery to sin into the freedom of being sons and daughters of God!

> For those who are led by the Spirit of God are the children of God. The Spirit you received does not make you slaves, so that you live in fear again; rather, the Spirit you received brought about your adoption to sonship. And by him we cry, "*Abba,* Father." The Spirit himself testifies with our spirit that we are God's children. (Romans 8:14–16 NIV)

Just as children who are adopted into a new family get all the benefits of belonging to that family, we who believe in Jesus get all the benefits of being adopted into God's family. God is no longer a distant ruler we have dishonored; he is our loving Father!

Our sanctification and adoption are connected. As adopted children who are being sanctified, we are growing and learning and becoming more and more like our Father. We can pray to him at any time. We can trust that he always wants what is best for his children. Sometimes our growth involves suffering, and in these times we can have confidence that our Father is still there holding us up.

Writer A. W. Tozer gives us a beautiful picture of God's smile as he looks at us—"the proud, tender smile of a Father who is bursting with pleasure over an imperfect but promising son who is coming every day to look more and more like the One whose child he is."[6]

WORDS TO KNOW

Sanctification: The process of growing and changing to be more like Christ.

DISCUSSION

Group members should take 5–6 minutes to look over the questions individually. Then the group should discuss the questions together (10 minutes).

1. What were the major things you learned or noticed as you read the passages from Romans 6, 8, and 12? (Feel free to look back at your notes!)

2. What is sanctification? What role does the Holy Spirit play in our sanctification?

3. How can knowing you are an adopted child of God change the way you live as a Christian today?

4. What challenges keep you from living in a way that fits your new identity?

SURVEY

We will conduct a survey about the church after our next session. For now, file away what you've learned about the new life believers have in Christ.

BELONGING TO THE FAMILY OF GOD

INTRODUCTION

Read this introduction aloud as a group (2–3 minutes).

Why Belonging Matters

Countless books and movies have told stories of children who have been orphaned. Many of these children have comical or mysterious or even magical adventures. But often these stories have something else in common besides an entertaining plot. Sometimes the main character feels that something is missing—they feel a keen desire to *belong*. Harry Potter is mistreated at his aunt and uncle's house but finds friends and a kind mentor at Hogwarts. Anne of Green Gables has an unhappy past in which her only friends are imaginary. But she finds a loving home with Matthew and Marilla Cuthbert, and there she is able to thrive.

Humans are hardwired to want to belong.

But sometimes we feel disconnected from people around us. Sometimes our relationships are shallow or awkward. Sometimes we want more from our parents, or our brothers and sisters, or our friends. Like some of these fictional characters, we feel like something is missing, and we long for a sense of deep and lasting belonging.

As we saw in the last session, through the gospel we have perfect, never-ending belonging to God. We have a perfect—and perfectly loving—heavenly Father, so we will never be alone.

But once we are adopted by God, we also gain a huge family of brothers and sisters, made up of everyone else God has graciously adopted!

Now the young person who feels her parents don't understand her can find encouragement and support in her family of faith. The student who scrolls away the boredom of life on his phone can find friendship with other believers. When we belong to Christ, we belong to each other.

Reading

Read the Bible passages together (4–6 minutes).

As you read each passage, think about what Paul's main point might be. You may wish to jot down some notes below.

- **Romans 8:14–17, 28–29**

- **Romans 12:1–18**

ARTICLE

Read this article aloud as a group (9–12 minutes).

NEW COMMUNITY

Over the last several weeks, we've read a lot from Paul's letters, especially his letter to the Romans. A chunk of the New Testament is made up of letters Paul wrote, and most of those letters are written to groups of people in various cities. In these letters, he is speaking not to individuals but to the community—brothers and sisters—a family. As Paul writes, he no doubt pictures them all gathered together to listen as his letter is read aloud.

So whatever he's explaining to his readers, whatever he's telling them to do—it's all being written to "you" plural. One easy way to think of this plural "you" is the Southern way: *y'all*. So in Romans 12:1 Paul is basically saying, "I urge y'all to present your bodies as a living sacrifice."

We call this *y'all*—this new community—by a familiar name: the church.

There are two ways in which we become part of the church when we repent and believe the gospel and are adopted into God's family. There is the *universal church* and the *local church*.

The *universal church* is the community of all true believers for all time.[7] We are not alone, but share an invisible connection with all the believers in Christ around the world and with all the believers from ages past. How awesome is that?

The *local church* is sometimes called the *visible* church. That is because it is the gathering of Christ-followers that we can actually see meeting together. The local church is where believers plug in and get to know one another.

A complete understanding of the gospel has to include an understanding of the church. Why? Because everyone who embraces the gospel is immediately born into the community of the church.

The church is our new home. Fellow believers are our new adoptive family. In the gospel, we are not just united to Christ, we are united to his church. We're all brothers and sisters. And, in a sense, Jesus is our big brother—Paul calls him "the firstborn among many brothers and sisters" (Romans 8:29).

Once we come to Christ in faith, we are called to connect with believers around us who will teach and encourage and walk alongside us as we all seek to become more like him.

We twenty-first century Christians often tend to prize individualism and independence. We need this gospel reorientation toward community. Jesus Christ died and rose again for *us*, not simply for *me*.

Listen to this urging from the book of Hebrews: "Let us hold tightly without wavering to the hope we affirm, for God can be trusted to keep his promise. Let us think of ways to *motivate one another* to acts of love and good works. And *let us not neglect our meeting together*, as some people do, but *encourage one another*, especially now that the day of his return is drawing near" (Hebrews 10:23–25 NLT, emphasis added).

The "hope we affirm" is the gospel. When we gather, we remember this good news together. When we spend time together, the Holy Spirit uses us in one another's lives, as we're all on the journey of sanctification. And we remind each other that God is at work in each of us as our loving Father!

THE BODY

We've examined how the church is a family.

But the Bible also describes the church as a body: "Just as our bodies have many parts and each part has a special function, so it is with Christ's body. We are many parts of one body, and we all belong to each other" (Romans 12:4–5 NLT).

The idea of a bunch of people making up one body might sound strange at first. But when you think about it, it starts to make sense. And that picture teaches us some important things about the new community we belong to.

Describing the church as a family, of course, conveys the ideas of togetherness and unity. But the picture of the church as a body takes the ideas of togetherness and unity to a new level—in fact, the members of the body are inseparable!

One point about the body that Paul really drives home is that even though it is *one* body, there is diversity within it. We don't all look alike. We don't all have the same personalities. We don't all have the same gifts or interests or experiences. But each one of us is a uniquely valuable part of the body:

> Yes, the body has many different parts, not just one part. If the foot says, "I am not a part of the body because I am not a hand," that does not make it any less a part of the body. And if the ear says, "I am not part of the body because I am not an eye," would that make it any less a part of the body? If the whole body were an eye, how would you hear? Or if your whole body were an ear, how would you smell any- thing? But our bodies have many parts, and God has put each part just where he wants it. . . . The eye can never say to the hand, "I don't need you." The head can't say to the feet, "I don't need you." In fact, some parts of the body that seem

weakest and least important are actually the most necessary. . . . This makes for harmony among the members, so that all the members care for each other. If one part suffers, all the parts suffer with it, and if one part is honored, all the parts are glad. (1 Corinthians 12:14–18, 21–22, 25–26 NLT)

And who is the head of this surprising body? Jesus! He is the one who guides and directs it. When people see the members of the body working together and loving one another, they should be able to see what Jesus himself is like. It is, after all, *his* body.

You read in Romans 12 about many ways in which the members of Christ's body are to be unified in love for one another: Don't think of yourself too highly. Use the gifts God has given you. Honor one another. Be patient. Pray. Share with one another. Show hospitality. Live in peace and harmony. Many of Paul's other letters have similar lists. In fact, unity among believers is so important to Jesus that he prayed about it shortly before he was crucified, and his prayer is recorded for us in the Gospel of John:

> "I pray not only for these [his disciples], but also for those who believe in me through their word. May they all be one, as you, Father, are in me and I am in you. May they also be in us, so that the world may believe you sent me. I have given them the glory you have given me, so that they may be one as we are one. I am in them and you are in me, so that they may be made completely one, that the world may know you have sent me and have loved them as you have loved me." (John 17:20–23)

Be encouraged! God doesn't want us to do life all alone. He has given us fellow members of his body to support us, and a family to love us, challenge us, and remind us of our new identity as much-loved children of God.

DISCUSSION

Group members should take 5–6 minutes to look over the questions individually. Then the group should discuss the questions together (10 minutes).

1. How does it change the way you think about church to see other believers as brothers and sisters who have also been adopted by grace into God's family?

2. Why is it important to be involved in a local church with other believers?

3. How is the body a helpful picture of the church?

4. In your life, what are the major challenges that keep you from living as you should within your new community, the church? Who or what can help you overcome those challenges?

5. How can you help the local church that you are part of become more like the one the Bible describes?

SURVEY

Survey two or three people by asking them the question below. Before beginning your conversations, review "Tips for Conducting Your Surveys" (p. 4). You will share what you found out the next time your group meets.

Write the answers people give you in the spaces below.

This week's question is *What do you think of when you hear the word* church?

Answers to this question might vary widely. Some people have had personal experiences with church that have flavored their view of Christ and Christians in one way or another. Others will be leaning on the experiences of their friends or family or on what they see and hear around them.

Whatever the case, once again be a LISTENER. The purpose of this question is to hear where people are coming from.

Person #1

What do you think of when you hear the word *church*?

Person #2

What do you think of when you hear the word *church*?

Person #3

What do you think of when you hear the word *church*?

Notes for Yourself:

What did you learn from your survey?

What connections do you see between the survey responses and the article or Scriptures you've been studying?

LOOKING AHEAD IN HOPE

INTRODUCTION

Read this introduction aloud as a group (2–3 minutes).

Why the Restoration of God's Kingdom Matters

In session 8 we discussed the *already* and the *not yet*. We are in Christ the moment we repent and believe the good news. God *already* grants us a new identity and welcomes us into a new community. But that's not the end of the story. The *not yet* is still to come! We are on a journey that leads us to a glorious future in God's restored kingdom.

Often people view the future in one of two ways.

You may have friends who have a worldview like the one in John Lennon's song "Imagine." Lennon dreams of a world with no possessions, no borders, no religions—just a brotherhood living as one. If we try hard enough to come together, he suggests, there will be less injustice, less hunger, less suffering. Now, in many times and places throughout history, people have tried to achieve this dream, yet they have not been able to eliminate human greed and selfishness and violence.

By contrast, you probably also have friends who look toward the future with no hope at all. When they observe the world around them, they see broken families and hatred and war and oppression and environmental devastation. As a result, they believe humanity is doomed.

How does the Christian vision of the future compare with these very different views?

First, it shares some similarities with Lennon's dream. But it's much more complete, and it's more realistic because it takes human nature into account.

Second, like your friends who see doom ahead, Christians can look clearly at the many things that are wrong with our world. But although the evil they see saddens them and spurs them to help people who are caught up in it, it doesn't leave them hopeless.

The difference is that Christians are able to look beyond what humans alone can accomplish. They turn their eyes to their good Creator and King. Injustice will be reversed by the perfect justice of a loving and righteous Judge. Hunger and suffering will be no more as everyone who trusts in Jesus enjoys eternal life and fellowship together with their Savior. The things Christ promises are the things your friends long for; human souls by nature want to get back to *shalom*, life as it should be, with our Creator. But what God promises is even "more than all we ask or imagine" (Ephesians 3:20 NIV).

Reading

Together, read these passages from the very last chapters of the Bible (4–6 minutes).

As you read, think about these questions: How are these final chapters an epic resolution to the story that began in Genesis? What are some specific ways various parts of the gospel story get wrapped up? Where do you see God still acting as the loving Creator, supreme authority, and final Judge? You may wish to jot down some notes below.

- **Revelation 20:10–15**

- **Revelation 21:1–11**

- **Revelation 21:22–22:5**

How are these final chapters an epic resolution to the story that began in Genesis? What are some specific ways various parts of the gospel story get wrapped up?

Notes:

Where do you see God still acting as the loving Creator, supreme authority, and final Judge?

Notes:

ARTICLE

Read this article aloud as a group (9–12 minutes).

When we arrive at the last scene in the book of Revelation, we find some familiar themes from the opening pages of Genesis: an angel, Satan (the serpent), human beings, the tree of life that is no longer out of reach, and more. Connections to the first three chapters of Genesis are everywhere.

And God and his goodness have the final victory! The darkest hour in history is followed by the dawn of a brilliant new day that will never end.

Two main events dominate these pages: final judgment and the re-creation of heaven and earth.

FINAL JUDGMENT

Revelation gives us a vivid picture of the future when we humans will stand before the Judge.

> Then I saw a great white throne and one seated on it. . . . I also saw the dead, the great and the small, standing before the throne, and books were opened. Another book was opened, which is the book of life, and the dead were judged according to their works by what was written in the books. Then the sea gave up the dead that were in it, and death and Hades gave up the dead that were in them; each one was judged according to their works. Death and Hades were thrown into the lake of fire. This is the second death, the lake of fire. And anyone

whose name was not found written in the book of life was thrown into the lake of fire. (Revelation 20:11–15)

The history of the whole world is about to reach its grand climax. We've been waiting for this day since Genesis 3—since the fall and God's promise of rescue!

Now in Revelation, the victorious King sits on his throne. This is the King of kings and Lord of lords, Jesus Christ. Before him stand all who have died—all people from the beginning of time. They stand before the one who lovingly created them, holds supreme authority, and is about to carry out his final judgment.

What is this judgment based on?

To answer that question, let's take a look at the books mentioned in Revelation 20. First, we read that "books were opened." What are these books? They contain a record of all humanity's deeds, yours and mine included. Every thought, word, and action of every human being has been recorded.

These words are haunting: "Each one was judged according to their works." On that day, people will stand in front of God with their mouths silent, guilty as charged.

But then a *different* book is mentioned: "Another book was opened, which is the book of life." What is contained in this Book of Life? Is it a bunch of good works to try to outweigh the bad works? Absolutely not! The final Judge does not weigh good deeds against bad deeds. The only thing recorded in the Book of Life is a list of names: the names of everyone who by grace, through faith in Christ's death and resurrection, are part of God's family.

If you are in Christ, you do not have to fear the day of judgment. Your name is in the Book of Life! "There is now no condemnation for those in Christ Jesus" (Romans 8:1). Because of the Great Exchange, our sins have been taken away. Instead of being condemned, those whose names are recorded in the Book of Life are welcomed into "a new heaven and a new earth" (Revelation 21:1). God brings his children home. No more death. No more sin. No more crying or pain. All that is gone. Forever.

Ponder those words. We have never lived in a world without death and the fear it brings. In our world, reminders of death are everywhere—both the sudden, shocking kinds and the slow, agonizing kinds. Oh, to live in that place where death is completely absent!

Wait—no more sin either? It is gone from my life, gone from my desires, gone from everyone else in the entire world. Astounding! Glorious! Whatever crying or pain there was as a result of death and sin—gone. Forever gone. We are in a whole new world.

And how about this: Have you ever thought, *I wonder what it would have been like to walk and talk with Jesus when he was here?* Well, you'll get that chance! Jesus himself will welcome you into this wondrous new home. HOME! What a homecoming, with all of our brothers and sisters from around the globe and from all of time! And at the head of the table is our Brother, who gave his life so we could be there.

I can't wait.

The hope of the gospel must go out to all. We want everyone to be with us in the new kingdom. But many people don't know that there will be a day when they will stand before the Judge. They need to know. And they need to know that they can have their sins taken away by Jesus. If they are "in Christ"—if they have been justified—they do not need to be afraid of that day. They, too, will be welcomed home.

NEW HEAVEN AND NEW EARTH

Then Jesus looks over all his redeemed people and with great joy cries, "Look, I am making everything new" (Revelation 21:5). And remember that tree Adam and Eve were guarded from after they sinned? The tree of life? Look at Revelation 22:1–2: "Then he showed me the river of the water of life, clear as crystal, flowing from the throne of God and of the Lamb [Jesus] down the middle of the city's main street. The tree of life was on each side of the river, bearing twelve kinds of fruit, producing its fruit every month."

The tree of life is alive, breathtaking, enormous! It spans a whole river and produces more and more incredible fruit every month!

What will we do in this new heaven and new earth? Do you recall what God wanted from the beginning? Adam was to reign over a perfect garden. Check out Revelation 22:5: "And they will reign forever and ever." All is as it should be. Eden is restored. And we get to be there.

I hope the fulfillment of the eternal gospel and the restoration of all good things fills you with wonder, worship, and deep gratitude. I also hope it fills you with an incredible desire to tell others what you have found.

DISCUSSION

Group members should take 5–6 minutes to look over the questions individually. Then the group should discuss the questions together (10 minutes).

1. How are the final chapters of the Bible an epic resolution to the Big Story of the Bible?

2. Often the end of a great story will tie together themes and ideas brought up in the beginning. What do you see in this passage that reminds you of Genesis 1–3?

3. What is the difference between "the books" and the Book of Life mentioned in the account of the judgment?

4. Whose names are written in the Book of Life? And how do those names get there?

5. Look again at the words used in Revelation to describe the new heaven and the new earth. How is the biblical picture different from the popular view of heaven?

6. We've seen a beautiful picture of the new kingdom that we'll experience as followers of Christ. How can we contribute to God's kingdom now while we wait for this ultimate ending?

7. Discuss what you have learned from this course.

NOTES FOR THE GROUP LEADER

Thank you for taking your group through this study!

Here is some advice that we hope will help your time in this study go more smoothly.

We recommend that you read the introduction to the book before starting to lead your group. It will orient you to the various parts of each lesson or "session."

In each session we have given the approximate amount of time we expect each portion to take. In general, most lessons should be able to be completed within about forty-five minutes. Allowing longer than forty-five minutes will, of course, permit more discussion—and we hope participants will want to discuss!—but we know that time is often limited. One little way to save time would be to print out the Bible readings in advance.

Most sessions will begin with a sharing time, when students share with one another what they learned from conducting their surveys. We have suggested that each student survey two people. If possible, these surveys should be done in person. However, you can judge what seems realistic to ask of the participants in your group. Each survey assignment includes a reminder for students to review "Tips for Conducting Your Surveys" (p. 4). You might want to add a verbal reminder as well because the tips include some important principles for listening well.

We recommend doing all the reading (the introduction to the session, the Bible reading, and the article) aloud, as a group. There are different ways you can approach this. You could go around the room and have students each read a paragraph or two for all three portions of reading. Or you could decide to read the introduction, which is shorter than the article, yourself. You could ask for volunteers to read larger chunks of Scripture. In short, you can decide what works best for your group. One suggestion: make sure reading aloud is voluntary. Some students are deeply uncomfortable reading in front of their peers. If you are going around the room having students take turns reading, you might want to tell them in advance that if they'd rather not read, they have the option to say "pass" and let the next student take over.

To help participants know what to look for when they are reading the Scripture passages, each Bible reading is accompanied by questions or prompts. There is also room for students to take notes if they find that helpful. Some questions prepare them for the discussion time later in the session, while others help them make connections to topics that have come up in earlier sessions.

On the topic of Bible readings, we recommend that you choose a relatively simple translation such as the Christian Standard Bible (csb), New International Version (niv), or New Living Translation (nlt). For dense theological passages like the readings from Romans, the NLT will make it a little easier for your participants to grasp the points Paul is making.

We hope that the time you and your students spend in *Gospel 101* will be thought-provoking and even life-changing!

ENDNOTES

Session 4

1. Timothy Keller, *The Prodigal God* (New York: Dutton, 2008), 43.

Session 6

2. R. C. Sproul's use of the three circles can be found, for example, in *The Truth of the Cross* (Lake Mary, FL: Reformation Trust, 2007), 85–95.

3. This is an adapted and shortened version of a story once told by Fred Barshaw, an elder at Grace Community Church in Sun Valley, CA. He had a gift for creating incredible parables, allegorical stories with deep biblical themes running through them.

Session 7

4. Craig S. Keener, *The IVP Bible Background Commentary: New Testament*, 2nd ed. (Downers Grove, IL: InterVarsity Press, 2014), 376.

5. John Stott, *Basic Christianity* (Downers Grove, IL: InterVarsity, 1971), 110.

Session 8

6. A. W. Tozer, *The Root of the Righteous* (Chicago: Moody, reprinted 2015), 20.

Session 9

7. Wayne Grudem, *Systematic Theology: An Introduction to Biblical Doctrine* (Grand Rapids, MI: Zondervan, 1994), 853.

"This book will equip students by taking them through a clear, easy-to-understand layout of the gospel, helping them be more confident to share the good news with those around them, including those who seem hostile to the faith."

Russell Moore, Editor in Chief, *Christianity Today*

"I'm thrilled to see this excellent resource published. It will help teenagers understand the gospel more fully and communicate it to others more effectively."

Bob Thune, Founding Pastor, Coram Deo Church, Omaha, NE; author of *Gospel Eldership* and coauthor of *The Gospel-Centered Life for Teens*

"Jeff Dodge is one of the most vibrant followers of Christ and one of the most committed Christian ministers I know. He is a man worth listening to, and *Gospel 101 for Teens* is a book I highly recommend reading."

Jason K. Allen, President, Midwestern Baptist Theological Seminary

"*Gospel 101 for Teens* is practical, scriptural, and engaging. Teens will walk away from this book with a clearer understanding of the gospel and a road map for sharing it with others. The story emphasis and the short-form layout break down complex concepts and keeps all students engaged. Get this in the hands of your student ministry!"

Vince Greenwald, Assistant Pastor of Youth and College, Immanuel Church Nashville